INSOMNIA

INSOMNIA

POEMS

LINDA PASTAN

W. W. NORTON & COMPANY
Independent Publishers Since 1923
New York | London

For information about permission to reproduce selections from this book,
write to Permissions, W. W. Norton & Company, Inc.,
500 Fifth Avenue, New York, NY 10110

For information about special discounts for bulk purchases, please contact
W. W. Norton Special Sales at specialsales@wwnorton.com or 800-233-4830

Manufacturing by LSC Communications Harrisonburg
Book design by Chris Welch
Production manager: Louise Mattarelliano

Library of Congress Cataloging-in-Publication Data

Pastan, Linda, date.
[Poems. Selections]
Insomnia : poems / Linda Pastan.
pages ; cm
ISBN 978-0-393-24718-3 (hardcover)
I. Title.
PS3566.A775A6 2015
811'.54—dc23
                              2015019106

ISBN 978-0-393-35375-4 pbk.

W. W. Norton & Company, Inc., 500 Fifth Avenue, New York, N.Y. 10110
www.wwnorton.com

W. W. Norton & Company Ltd., 15 Carlisle Street, London W1D 3BS

1 2 3 4 5 6 7 8 9 0

FOR IRA

CONTENTS

1

COUNTING SHEEP

2

SHIP'S CLOCK

3

MUSINGS BEFORE SLEEP

ACKNOWLEDGMENTS

I would like to thank the following magazines in which many of these poems first appeared:

The American Scholar; The Atlantic; Catamaran; Bellevue Literary Review; Five Points; The Gettysburg Review; The Georgia Review; Great River Review; The Jung Journal; The Kenyon Review; Moment; New Letters; The New Yorker; Nimrod; The Paris Review; Plume; Poet Lore; Prairie Schooner; The Southern Poetry Review; Virginia Quarterly Review.

"Elizabethan" appeared in *Shakespeare's Sisters*, published by the Folger Shakespeare Library.

"In the Happo-en Garden, Tokyo" was featured on the American Academy of Poets' Poem-A-Day.

1

COUNTING SHEEP

INSOMNIA: 3 AM

Sleep has stepped out
for a smoke
and may not be back.

The sun is waiting
in the celestial
green room,

practicing
its flamboyant
entrance.

In the hour of the wolf
there is only
the clock

for company,
ticking
through the dark

remorseless
stations
of the night.

COSMOLOGY

Someone has spilled the moon
all over the trees;

someone is cutting down the trees,
branch by forked branch—

soon there will be nothing left
but kindling.

Why am I afraid of the dark
but more afraid of what the light reveals:

this moonlight which lies everywhere
like a beautiful torn shroud;

the illumination of dreams, room
after room of dreams?

Is it the moon itself I fear,
in too many pieces now

to put back together? Or the stars,
light-years away, my voice

traveling towards them
in a blind trajectory?

I fear the earth as it warms
and freezes; I fear your arms

which hold me a moment
and disappear.

CONSIDER THE SPACE
BETWEEN STARS

Consider the white space
between words on a page, not just
the margins around them.

Or the space between thoughts:
instants when the mind is inventing
exactly what it thinks

and the mouth waits
to be filled with language.
Consider the space

between lovers after a quarrel,
the white sheet a cold metaphor
between them.

Now picture the brief space
before death enters, hat in hand:
these vanishing years, filled with light.

FIRST SNOW

The clouds dissolve in snow—
a simple act of physics
or the urge to just let go?

On hills, on frozen lakes
all definition fades
before the rush of flakes

until, bereft of light,
the moon gives up
her sovereign claim to white.

THE GARDENER

He's out rescuing his fallen hollies
after the renegade snowstorm,

sawing their wounded limbs off
quite mercilessly (I think of the scene

in *Kings Row*, the young soldier waking
to find his legs gone).

He's tying up young bamboo—
their delicate tresses litter the driveway—

shoveling a door through the snow
to free the imprisoned azaleas.

I half expect him to tend his trees
with aspirin and soup, the gardener

who finds in destruction
the very reason to carry on;

who would look at the ruins
of Eden and tell the hovering angel

to put down his sword,
there was work to be done.

COUNTING SHEEP

Counting sheep, the scientists suggested, may
simply be too boring to do for very long, while
images of a soothing shoreline . . . are engrossing
enough to concentrate on.

—*The New York Times*

When I reach
a thousand
I start to notice
how the eyes
of one ewe are wide,
as if with worry
about her lamb
or how cold
the flock will be
after the shearing.
At a thousand fifty
I notice a ram
pushing up against
a soft and curly female,
and for a moment
I'm distracted by errant
images of sex.
It's difficult
to keep so many sheep
in line for counting—
they are not a parade
but more like a roiling
sea of whitecaps,
which makes me think
of the shore—

of all those boring
grains of sand
to keep track of
as they slip
through the fingers,
of all the dangers
of sunstroke,
riptide, jellyfish.
The scientists fall
asleep lulled
by equations,
dreaming
of test tubes.
I fall asleep
at last by
counting them:
biologist,
physicist,
astronomer,
and all the many
experts
on the subject
of sleep.

ECLIPSE

Moon, half rusted away
in the sun's indomitable shadow,

I stand at the frosted window
wrapped in a flannel robe

and see not what Galileo saw—
a universe of planets spinning

like plates from the hands
of a master juggler—

but you, our one moon,
slender at times,

at times full as a breast
brimming with milky light.

If the sun is a warrior
in flaming armor,

the moon is a ghost
disappearing,

leaving behind
the merest trace of stars.

METEOR SHOWER

Lying on our backs together
in the cool August grass

under a sky already starry
to the very rind,

we wait to be drenched
in light, for shooting stars—

those pinballs on the table of heaven—
to careen by,

for a shower of gold,
like Zeus descending

on the Danaë
with only lust in mind.

DERECHO

Our sleepy, domesticated earth
with its valleys and
flowers, looped ribbons

of river, voluptuous
clouds, awakens
after a long sleep

shaking itself
and with a roar (wild
beast after all) sends

houses, hilltops,
tree trunks spilling
off its rough back.

ROOT BALL

An asteroid has landed in our garden,
or a giant brain, ripped from its skull—
this monstrous root ball torn
from the ground when the poplar
it fed was assaulted by wind.
The workmen had to saw for days,
hauling the wood away with backhoes.
Now it simply lies there,
filled with soil and ropy vegetation:
a breast—great nourisher—without
its body, a bruised fist
without its arm, a giant ball
of yarn with lengths of root,
like knitting needles, sticking out,
pointing in all directions:
to the labyrinthine subway rumbling
under city streets, to the secret map
of blood under the skin.

THE BLACKBIRDS

I can only call it post
post modern—this music

let loose by the blackbirds
as they swarm south

abandoning trees—
those leafy songbooks—

like individual notes
gone mad.

And the woods ring
with the first sounds

of autumn, raucous
and dark,

before a single
leaf has changed.

DIDO AND AENEAS:
AFTER PURCELL

When Dido embraced
her own sword, she left
Aeneas behind

founding his city,
while she became
a different kind of legend,

no longer the understudy
to her own life—the queen
of abandoned women—

no longer a lonely solo but
the better part of a duet.
And voices would sing it,

would inscribe her beauty
note by note
into the scrolled music

of air, would tell how
her final marriage bed
was fire, fire, fire.

CASSANDRA

There are so few of them
at first
a mere rustle

on the wind
with just a hint of red
or gilt along their edges,

and the mother woods
are still green,
and the sun still spills

its molten light
on upturned faces;
no one worries

if a few are falling—
they are simply
grace notes,

wisps of portent,
though soon they turn
acrobatic

showing their bellies
to the breeze,
soon a few more

wordlessly
shake loose—early soldiers
of the season,

no smoke yet,
no raging flames
of color.

But make no mistake,
something is coming
to an end.

Pillars of fire?
The trees in autumn.

One small flame?
Head of a

woodpecker
at the feeder.

The wind is nothing
but blind

acceleration,
blowing us over

October's rough-hewn
threshold.

IN THE ORCHARD

Why are these old, gnarled trees
so beautiful, while I am merely
old and gnarled?

If I had leaves, perhaps, or apples . . .
if I had bark instead
of this lined skin,

maybe the wind would wind itself
around my limbs
in its old sinuous dance.

I shall bite into an apple
and swallow the seeds.
I shall come back as a tree.

A BRIEF HISTORY OF
HURRICANE LEE

1.

A minute before 5 am,
the alarm clock slumbering
in its bed of numbers,
I wait for the storied wind
and think of the quahog, snug
in its house
of shell, as the gull
approaches.

2.

I hear the throb
of a hammer
over the beating
of the rain.
My neighbor nailing
canvas to his split roof,
or Noah making
preparations?

3.

In the aftermath,
the hollies with
their green leaves lean
all the way over,
as though they were
listening for something
through a door
in the air.

ELEGY

Our final dogwood leans
over the forest floor

offering berries
to the birds, the squirrels.

It's a relic
of the days when dogwoods

flourished—creamy lace in April,
spilled milk in May—

their beauty delicate
but commonplace.

When I took for granted
that the world would remain

as it was, and I
would remain with it.

LATE IN OCTOBER

Late in October, I watch
it all unravel—the whole
autumn leafery
succumbing to rain.
At the moment
of their most intense beauty,
reds and yellows bleed
into each other
like dried paints on a palette—
those ghosts of pictures
never painted.

Perhaps beauty
is the mother of death,
not the other way around.
Perhaps the rain itself
is an answer: knives
of crystal, cleansing
and killing as it falls.
I turn from the window;
winter is coming next.
White will have
its own perfections.

AFTER THE SNOW

I'm inside
a Japanese woodcut,

snow defining
every surface:

shadows
of tree limbs

like pages
of inked calligraphy;

one sparrow,
high on a branch,

brief as
a haiku.

Here
in the Maryland woods, far

from Kyoto
I enter Kyoto.

2

SHIP'S CLOCK

SHIP'S CLOCK

The ship's clock, stowed in a box
for its passage to the beach each summer,
continues to chime every four hours
(first watch ... dog watch ...)
inside the cedar closet.

I look up from my desk and wonder
what that rounded sound could be,
then remember the clock,
all polished brass, still marking
the watches of a distant ocean.

So a prisoner might sing,
alone in a cell; or the songbird
serenade bright fronds
of leaf and fern, though caged
in the dark of a northern city.

The bird has its arias,
the clock its mathematics.
I string words together
wherever I am—
in planes, in waiting rooms,

forcing the actual to sink
and disappear
beneath the bright
and shimmering surface
of the half-imagined.

THE POETS

They are farmers, really—
hoeing and planting

in strict rows ripe with manure,
coaxing each nebulous seed

to grow. Year after year
of drought or rainstorm,

locust or killing frost, they bundle
their hay into stacks

of inflammable gold, or litter
the barn floors with empty husks.

At the market they acknowledge
each other gruffly and move on,

noting who has the more bountiful
harvest, whose bushel baskets

are laden with beets and tomatoes,
tumescent with fruit.

Under the sheen of success
or the long shadow of failure,

what they labor for remains
the same: their own muscular

beanstalk rocketing skyward
from a single bean.

GODS' MAN

a novel in woodcuts by Lynd Ward, 1939

When I was twelve I found it
on my parents' shelf: a fable
in black and white—the grain
of the wood caught by the ink—
a fugue for those hard times: look
of the Bauhaus, climate of Grimm.
It gave me fascinated nightmares.

And that skull on the last page
grinning as it claimed the soul
it had bargained for. The currency:
pure genius in the shape
of a wand—paintbrush
or pen as long as an arm.
Think of the not quite innocent

longings of the artist who wanted
not just to have but to make it all,
searching the streets of the city
with its whores and its moneymen.
And who was Gods' man anyway,
the painter or the stand-in
for that fallen angel Lucifer?

What could it have meant
to me at twelve, barely an adolescent?
What might I have given,
what would I give, for those wild
moments of perfect beauty
in painting or poem, beyond
even the intention of the maker?

AND EVENING:
FOR ROLAND FLINT

Here you are, alive
on the page
years after your death,

though that's an immortality
you might have traded
for one cold beer tonight

or the honeyed embrace
of a girl just half imagined
even then.

Immortality
and its bastard brother
fame—you wanted both

even as you scorned them,
those evenings
we talked for hours

about the purgatory
of neglect; that year
when our fledgling books

were shaped not like coffins
but like coffers
of Keatsian gold.

REMEMBERING STAFFORD
ON HIS CENTENNIAL

When you said there was no such thing
as writer's block if your standards
were low enough, everyone laughed
and I laughed too, but you meant it, didn't you?

The point is to follow the winding path
of words wherever it wants to take you, step
by step, ignoring the boulders, the barbed wire
fences, the rutted ditches choked with ragweed.

How complicated such simplicities are.
Forget the destination, you taught us,
forget applause; what matters is the journey.
And started one yourself, each morning.

ELIZABETHAN

Some gentler passion slide into my mind,
For I am soft and made of melting snow
—Queen Elizabeth I

Her sex sent her mother
to the tower,
made her father profligate
with arrogant desires,

but she was made of flint
and backbone.

Think of a young girl
in a blue velvet bodice,
a white collar and lace,
the very prototype
of virginal.

Think of a woman, her court
enlivened by suitors and lovers
in doublets, in brocaded cloaks,
despite suspicions of their motives
staining the sheets

the way cups of spicy,
flowery mead were sipped
despite the possibility
of poison.

Even the crown of the sun
must go down each night.

Could she have stood at the prow
of a ship in that great Armada she ordered,

instead of at a window, waiting
for urgent results?

Could she have guessed that the words
of a man she inspired, carved
into the marble of ages,
had a muscular beauty
more than equal
to her own worldly triumphs?

Daughter, Queen, Ruler
of roiling seas, of meandering
rivers and meadows,
of armies of soldiers, their swords
and armor glittering
like planets to her sun.

Namesake to an age.

And Poet?
When she turned
to the empty parchment
(or once to a windowpane,
a diamond for quill)
everything
must have gone quiet.

Even a queen is naked
before the naked page, awaiting
not the generous spoils owed to a victor
but the gifts freely given
of a besotted muse.

ON INSTALLING ANNE BRADSTREET IN THE CATHEDRAL OF ST. JOHN THE DIVINE, POETS' CORNER

What would Mistress Bradstreet think
of this stony urban cathedral—
incense prickling the nostrils,

misting the eye—of these golds
and scarlets, gilts and velvets, this
so ceremonial ceremony?

And what would my grandfather
think, leaning on banks of cloud
as on extra pillows Passover night,

watching from his strict Jewish heaven
as I follow a priest and his crucifix
down the lengthy exacting aisle?

I'm celebrating Poetry,
installing our sisterly muse
the way Wordsworth and Lamb

were installed in Westminster Abbey,
across that turbulent ocean
Anne herself once bravely sailed.

Still, I'd rather think of her beside
the dear and loving husband she desired
(more ardently than her prickly Puritan

minister required or would have condoned)
kneeling in a plain wooden church
the white of a new England winter.

AT THE END OF THE 19TH CENTURY

A boneyard of old poems
rusts away, stanza

by creaking stanza.
Odes lose their polish;

couplets are torn
apart. And in a fertile

land, the odor
of free verse seeps

into the groundwater.

FLORA

In the great Archaeological Museum of Naples,
I visited Flora—force
behind everything that flowers—a fresco
rescued from buried Pompeii
in the 18th century.

I knew I had seen her before:
her pastel mood, her delicate
veils embroidered with blossom,
those pale limbs, her hair streaming
with the essence of flowers.

It must have been in Botticelli's *Primavera*,
a train ride away in the Uffizi,
as if an artist of the 16th century
had envisioned the walls of Pompeii
long before he could have seen them.

In the same room in Naples, stood the hollow wooden cow
Daedalus fashioned for Queen Pasiphaë to hide in,
waiting for her lover, that muscled bull.
Centuries later in Shakespeare,
another queen would think she loved an ass.

So artists dip into a deep but circumscribed pool,
fishing for something new
but sometimes finding
(still dripping with beauty)
the indelible, unknowable familiar.

ON THE ROAD TO POMPEII

On the Road to Pompeii, our taxi driver
points out a small house on the slopes of Vesuvio.
"I live there," he says, "I grow a few grapes—
volcano sweet—and I can sell you some.
I once was in Chicago," he tells us next
in his musically staccato English.
"People had guns there, more dangerous
than volcanoes," and he laughs.

I ask him if he's worried, living so close
to the peak. He sighs and shakes his cigarette
out the window, the miniature ash
a kind of synopsis of what a volcano
could do if it liked. "What can I tell you?
You live where you have to live."

Nothing has changed in Naples
in the ten years I've been gone.
The traffic snarls to the same halt,
and tourists will still be lined up
in Pompeii to see the shell of a girl caught
as she fled so many centuries ago,
the lava pursuing her like some TV monster.
"You have to burn to shine," observes
the theme song of *The Sopranos*.

Vesuvio is an expensive view now.
The hotels charge more if you can see it
from your room, a peaceful-looking dragon
holding its fiery breath, biding its time.

CHAOS THEORY

Our butterfly bush
(*Buddleia* or
summer lilac)

is hung with clusters
of blossoms, clusters
of butterflies the color

of blossoms:
Tiger Swallowtails,
Red-spotted Admirals,

fluttering Cabbage Whites
engraved in an
inky hieroglyphic.

At times their wings are folded
like the covers
of a book

that opens suddenly
and comes to life
with language.

And if what I've read
is true, I'm looking at
the first small flickering—

one hinged wing, perhaps—
the tiny movement
of a force

that will grow
and cascade
across oceans and

time zones, barreling on
and on until somewhere
an army of soldiers,

oiling their guns
as they wait for a break in
the weather, look up

at the clearing sky—
clouds the color of milkweed—
and like the god Mithras,

ancient namesake
to the butterfly,
prepare for battle.

EDWARD HOPPER, UNTITLED

An empty theatre: seats
shrouded in white
like rows of headstones;
the curtain about to rise
(or has it fallen?)
on a scene
of transcendental
silence.

And the audience?
A solitary figure sheathed
in black, a woman
in a hat perhaps
(more abstract
shape than woman)
sitting alone
in the cavernous dark.

This is quintessential Hopper—
cliché of loneliness
transformed by brushstroke
into something part paint,
part desperation.
"Oil on board," the label says,
as if even a tree
had to be sacrificed.

ADAM AND EVE, BY
LUCAS CRANACH THE ELDER, 1526

She seems a mere girl really,
small-breasted and slim,
her body luminescent
next to Adam, who scratches
his head in mild perplexity.
So many baubles hang
from the tree
it didn't hurt to pick one.
The snake is a quicksilver curve
on a branch she is almost
young enough to swing from.

The garden bores her anyway—
no weedy chaos among
the flowers and vegetables;
the animals so tame
you can hardly tell the lamb
from the lion, the doe from the stag
whose antlers outline Adam's modesty.
She is like that teen-age girl
who wandered from the mall last week
not to be seen again, the world before her
glittering and perilous.

THE CONSERVATION OF MATTER

A flurry of leaves at the window
like those calendar pages flying
in old movies
to indicate time passing,
and it is passing,
though where it's going
nobody seems to know.

Something is always lost
and something found—
an earring or the key
to a certain door,
to some second self.
I watch as energy and matter
bow and switch places,
as last year's leaves appear
and disappear again

like my childhood room
with its billowy curtains
and the picture of orange horses
with blue manes hanging over my bed—
I thought it was gone,

but I walked through
The Marc Museum last month
and there it was, the very picture.
And the child I was,
still hiding in this body,
rose up in recognition.

THE BRIDGE

At Loew's Burnside Theatre in the forties
an unknown boy pressed his face
to mine. We were in the children's section;
a glowering matron patrolled the aisles alert
as a watchdog, nose twitching, for noise
or fighting or missiles of wadded gum.
Not for the discovery of desire
by twelve-year-old strangers,
The Bridge of San Luis Rey looming
on the screen, Akim Tamiroff starring.
I still remember that bridge (woven by Incas
imagined by Thornton Wilder) falling
and falling, the actors in period costume spilling
like tenpins into space, caught in midair
as I was, partway between love and death.

REPETITIONS:
AFTER VAN GOGH

1. YELLOW

When the yellow bird—
a finch maybe—swept
up through the trees

I thought for a moment
it was just another leaf,
a yellow leaf refusing to fall,

deserter from the great autumn
army—silent legions
in full retreat.

But it was just a bird,
a yellow bird,
possibly a finch.

2. RED

When the red bird—
a cardinal perhaps—flew
up through the trees

I thought for a minute
it was just another leaf,
a red leaf refusing to fall,

rebel from the great autumn
migration—silent exiles
in full retreat.

But it was just a bird,
a red bird,
probably a tanager.

3. WHITE

Something white moved
among the tangled branches
of the tree.

It could have been
a piece of moon
falling,

lighting up
the restless autumn
leaves.

But it was just a bird,
a white bird,
a dove, I think.

EXERCISE

Asked for an exercise—by a student, an editor working on a
book about writing, a fellow teacher—I mention two people
coming out of a building.

—Alice Mattison

Two people come out of a building—
not out of a bar, not a priest and rabbi.
Out of a church, perhaps, after a wedding,
the steeple white and bridal,

or out of a bank with stolen money spilling
in green confetti from their pockets,
a youngish man and woman
in homemade masks,

or from a house on fire, stories behind them
blazing; stories growing like wildfire
in the forest of prose. But when
two people leave a building in a poem

the building could be the body
and the two: flesh and spirit; or it could
be the universe itself, Earth
and its moon spinning from the galaxy.

I'll take prose. I'll put myself to sleep
with stories as real as a mother and father
lying in the next room dreaming, as they prepare
to leave the building of my life.

3

MUSINGS

BEFORE SLEEP

FIREFLIES

here come
the fireflies

with their staccato
lights

their tiny headlamps
blinking

in silence
through the tall grass

like constellations
cut loose

from the night
sky

(see how desire
transforms

the plainest
of us)

or flashes of insight
that flare

for a moment
then flicker out

IN THE HAPPO-EN
GARDEN, TOKYO

The way a birthmark
on a woman's face defines
rather than mars
her beauty,

so the skyscrapers—
those flowers of technology—
reveal the perfection
of the garden they surround.

Perhaps Eden is buried
here in Japan,
where an incandescent
koi slithers snakelike

to the edge of the pond;
where a black-haired
Eve-san in the petaled
folds of a kimono

once showed her silken body
to the sun, then picked a persimmon
and with a small bow
bit into it.

IMAGINARY CONVERSATION

You tell me to live each day
as if it were my last. This is in the kitchen
where before coffee I complain
of the day ahead—that obstacle race
of minutes and hours,
grocery stores and doctors.

But why the last? I ask. Why not
live each day as if it were the first—
all raw astonishment, Eve rubbing
her eyes awake that first morning,
the sun coming up
like an ingénue in the east?

You grind the coffee
with the small roar of a mind
trying to clear itself. I set
the table, glance out the window
where dew has baptized every
living surface.

LOVE POEM AGAIN

there are times when
anything feels
like a love poem

standing on line at the post office
for instance
waiting to lick

a stamp
I will buy with
the last loose

change in my pocket
(my own dna
anointing

the envelope)
so I can send you
this message

SEX EDUCATION

When a bee enters the plant's electric field, a small electric charge develops . . .
—Eartheasy blog

I remember what happened the day we met.
Electricity, they call it, a spark

like the one that went from God's finger
to Adam's in the Sistine Chapel.

I always thought it was a metaphor,
but now I read that bees are led to pollen

by a flower's electric force field,
not just by seductive reds and purples.

I remember how you looked at me,
how I looked back.

And spreading through my limbs
a sweetness, like honey.

COMMENCEMENT ADDRESS

If you live on the cutting edge,
surely you'll get cut.

If you live the simple life,
it won't be simple.

If you sit at a desk composing words
the alphabet will mock you,

or you'll drown in the currents
of the page.

Work hard. Be lazy.
Money will come and go

like green leaves in their season.
But don't forget

the wise man and the fool
are blood brothers.

At the end
what matters

is the sun, the moon:
arterial red, bone white.

NECKLACE

Each couplet should be a poem in itself, like a pearl in a
necklace . . .
 —"The Ghazal," by Len Anderson

If each couplet should represent a single pearl,
are these strung beads at my throat words disguised as pearls?

The hooked fish looks up at them with recognition
as his eyes fade to the opacity of pearls.

When I was young I wandered in Hawthorne's landscape
but didn't comprehend the innocence of Pearl.

In the spinning galaxy of the family,
the youngest has always been considered the pearl.

Irritation is the dark underside of love.
Just ask the oyster his method for making pearls.

Would one go to a death by water willingly,
believing Prospero's sea change: eyes into pearls?

Dusk steals up on them as they sit, barely talking,
under a shadowy sky, all mother-of-pearl.

If a perfect woman is worth more than rubies,
am I, so far from perfection, worth less than pearls?

MRI

Strapped down on my back
in a sci-fi spacecraft,
I wait, like an astronaut,
for liftoff. The mission:
to find the insidious comet
or meteor about to ruin
my hapless body.

Assaulted now
by sound (cymbals, cannons,
rat-tat-tat of firearms) and lost
in magnetic fields, I long
not for health but for simple quiet:
the storied silence
of outer space.

COURSE OF TREATMENT

After forty visits, after forty
invisible rays transformed
your body into something
as incandescent as a flashbulb,
they release you into

the world, where it hardly rained
those forty days, those nights, where
your ark was an old SUV shuttling you
back and forth along meandering
highways, taking their daily toll.

Now you embrace the ordinary again—
this small snow shower on the windshield,
which seems in its brevity
to have special meaning—
a shower of angel feathers perhaps,

or the bottle of wine we will
uncork in celebration,
its brothers waiting in a basement
redolent of the earth
you've once again escaped.

AT THE EDGE

We are having tea at the edge of the abyss . . .
—Raymond Farina

It's a long way down
to darkness and fire

and the wings of night birds
making unruly sounds.

To dismantled clocks.
To shoes filled with tears

and garments torn
in boredom and grief.

But here at the edge
of the abyss

the tea is the amber color
of comfort,

the biscuits are crisp
and sweet

as you feed them to me
with loving hands.

RIVER PIG

"So you like fugu," his Japanese host remarked
after my husband unwittingly ate the sushi
which can kill if not cleaned properly. River pig
it's also called. I'm glad I wasn't there.
But I remember a dinner where I preemptively
told my mushroom-gathering host
I was allergic to mushrooms. When he served
the cultivated kind I love, I had to refuse them.

And I remember puffer fish we caught and ate at the beach—
those distant relatives to fugu, though I didn't know it then.
The mushrooms that grow in our woods now
are every shape and size: the honey fungus and the hen-of-the-woods,
the smoky bracket. Some are as short and tough
as bruised thumbs, some like tiny fringed umbrellas.
They cling to trees or bivouac their armies on the grass.
Often they sprout like bad thoughts, overnight.

But under a canopy of fallen leaves, the delicate
chanterelles also hide, which people fry
in sizzling butter and devour. I never dared.
How well the dangerous can camouflage itself—
the temper that flares like lightning
from a sunny disposition; the switchblade
hiding in a well-tailored pocket.
Some women like a hint of danger in their men,

as sexy as the edge the thought of crashing
gives skydivers. I've always chosen safety.
But I'm haunted now (too late) by what I've missed:
that trip down a green and sinuous river. The man I said no to.
I don't eat raw fish. I choose the most benign (entombed
in plastic) mushrooms. As if I want to arrive at death
quite safe from harm, and innocent, locking the coffin lid
behind me so nothing dangerous can get in.

FINGERPRINTS

If you sign up for Global Entry, you can skip the long security
lines at airports and will not have to remove your jacket or
shoes.

—*Travel* magazine

I'm asked questions about travel—
what countries I've visited, how long I stayed.

They press my fingers to a pad then frown
and shake their heads and press again.

They say I have no fingerprints.
(Have I lost them? simply misplaced them?)

They say my skin is smooth as glass—
no grooved lines, no patterns.

I've finally become anonymous—
a wave whose ribbed imprint on the sand

has washed away as whorls do in emptying bathtubs,
sucked down the drain, leaving nothing behind.

I'm free now to rob houses,
commit murders leaving no trace.

(My love, if I caress you in the dark, will it seem
as if a knife blade has touched you?)

I'll wear mittens, clench my fists.
I'll hide my hands in my pockets

as if they were untrained animals.
As if they were tiny terrorists themselves.

OLD JOKE

The children all are grown, the dog has died;
the old joke says that now life can begin,
the creaking door to freedom open wide.
But old age seems my fault, a kind of sin
precluding guilty pleasures—food and drink,
the luxuries of travel, even books.

Depression is the bed in which I sink,
my body primed for pain's insidious hooks:
the swollen fingers and the stiffened back;
the way regret can pierce you with its knife;
the migraines like some medieval rack;
the winnowing of loved ones from my life.

For months I carried that old dog around
helping her eat and cleaning up her mess.
Though she was deaf, I talked to her—each sound
the rough equivalent of a caress.
If memories are like the poems I wrote
but didn't think quite good enough to save,

and if the final wisdoms I would quote
await that cold anthology: the grave,
then let the sun, at least, become a shawl
keeping me wrapped in warmth until the end;
my lawn a place where children's children sprawl
next to the shy ghost of my canine friend.

GHOSTS

We abandon the dead. We abandon them.
—Joseph Fasano

We abandon the dead as they
abandoned us. But sometimes
my mother's ghost sits at the foot of the bed

trying to comfort me for all
the other losses: my father longing
to be forgiven, to forgive;

the long line of cousins and aunts
patiently waiting their turns
to be remembered; the dogs

who were my shadows once
whining now at the gates of the afterlife.
My mother smooths my pillow

as though it were a field of snow
ready to be plowed by dreams where
for brief moments my dead come back:

Jon as a toddler in my uncle's army cap,
Franny with the rosary of days
slipping through her fingers.

At times I wander through
the library of graves, reading
the headstones, remembering a place

where the ashes I scattered once
blew back on the wind, staining
my forehead with their dark alphabet.

In the house where I grew up,
the same sentinel trees
shade the porch

as they shaded the green years
of my childhood when my dead
were alive and full of promise.

THE GRANDFATHERS

They hid in barbershops,
in steam baths, in shuls,
and on the benches
of small concrete parks,
spending their few
remaining coins of laughter
on each other, swallowing
humiliation, like schnapps,
in one gulp.

But tears were there
like secret tidal pools
doomed by salt. Though
once they had discarded
the villages of their fathers,
here they remained strangers,
choosing the enigmatic life
of fish or bees—silence
or that low dangerous hum.

CHOOSING SIDES

In the war between the flowers
and the deer, my husband
has chosen sides, putting up a fence
at which two doe briefly stand,
looking in, locked out
in the wide world.

And though our woods
are newly filled with flowers,
safe now on their stems,
I think continually
of the deer who sleep
like penitents on their knees.

AT MAHO BAY:
FOR JON

The pelicans are putting on a show—
breakfast for them means some poor fish must die.
We search the wreaths of coral far below

where golden hamlets flutter, blueheads glow,
all of it sweetest nectar for the eye,
while pelicans are putting on their show.

Is it amnesia these brief days bestow
on you and me whose lives are speeding by?
We search the reefs of coral far below

forgetting for the moment what we know
of illness, wintry weeping, of goodbye.
The pelicans are putting on a show.

The sand between our fingers seems to flow
as through an hourglass: time can only fly.
We search the wreaths of coral far below.

A plane is waiting, is it time to go?
Was so much turquoise beauty just a lie?
The pelicans are putting on a show.
We searched the wreaths of coral far below.

THE HIRED MOURNER

To hired mourners grief is good . . .
—*San Diego Tribune*

She sits beside the coffin
as they did in ancient
Greece and Rome,
keeping the body company,
keeping each shuddering
candle flame alight, guarding
the portal between this life
and whatever is next.

She wrings her hands (like wringing
out the wash) trying to mourn
the stranger lying there, remote
in his final traveling clothes,
the skull beneath his skin rising
to the surface as surely as the moon's
white skull rises at the window,
snuffing out innocent stars.

She mourns instead the stranger
she is to herself, sitting up all night
for stingy wages. But grief is good,
she read somewhere, it scours the soul
and is the only work she knows.
Her eyes rest on the coffin—
that silk-lined boxcar to eternity.
She thinks of her own losses:

a love she squandered once;
a mother and father who mourned
each other all their married life;
a terrier, the pick of the litter.
In the morning walking to the bus stop,
April flourishing around her,
she'll mourn the new green leaves
with scarcely half a year left in them.

AH, FRIEND

in the black hood,
come! Pierce
my heart

with the sharp ring
of the doorbell;
throw pebbles

at my window
with the perilous sound
of hail on a tin roof.

No more of these
odd hints: a feather
of blood here,

a shadow, the size
of a thumbprint,
on an X-ray there.

I will never be more ready
than I am now,
as I sit

peeling a tangerine
and turning the brittle pages
in the long book

of my life. I won't
even need to pack
for the journey.

LAST RITES

She's given up sex.
She's given up travel.
She's given up the rush
of alcohol to the brain
at the first sip of wine—
that sweet burn
as it slips down the throat.
And her quarrels,
her celebrations,
she's given them up too
as she's given up books—
their pages too heavy to turn.
What's left is a blur
of sky where the weather
rehearses its own finales.
What's left is blue emptiness
behind the white sail
of the nurse's starched cap,
steering her out to sea.

The lines on my face are starting
to make me look like photographs
of Auden in old age. If the lines
of my poems could also be
as incandescent as his,
would I be willing to look
as worn and wrinkled?
I avoid mirrors now,
particularly when the strong light
of morning reveals what I don't wish to see,
and sometimes I want to erase
the words I'm putting down,
even as my pen touches
the paper. Sometimes I feel guilty
about growing old and forgetful
and sometimes guilty about spending
so much time tinkering with language,
though tinkering isn't the word
most writers would use—revision,
we say, which is sometimes holy,
and also something many women do:
revise their faces with rouge or stitches.
Are there two kinds of vanity—
vanity about the beauty
we are born with or without,
and vanity about the beauty
we try to make out of the sticks
and stones of language?
Old age should be a time
of accepting the hand dealt out,

in fact already almost played out.
But in these moments when sleep
is about to take me, when I might be
any age at all, I think again of Auden who,
for the length of a dream at least,
may hold my all too human head
in the hands that wrote those poems.